CSU Poetry Series VII

THE
NARROWS

by Valery Nash

Cleveland State University Poetry Center

ACKNOWLEDGMENTS

Some of these poems have appeared or will appear in the following publications, to which grateful acknowledgment is made.

Artemis: "In Our Sixties"
Green House: "The Floral Dress"
Hollins Critic: "In Silks"
Mill Mountain Review: "My Child"
New South Writing: "Absence," "The Angle of Reflection" (originally titled "Sun Climbing"), "Traveller"
Pacific Moana Quarterly (New Zealand): "Rue de Monceau" (originally titled "Mother"), "The Smell," "The Woman Who Once Played God"
Poetry Northwest: "The Bike," "Patterning"
Poetry: Points of Departure (Winthrop, 1974): "Working for Doctor No"
Samphire (England): "At Eighty," "The Red Queen," "The Stones at Devereux"
Southern Poetry Review: "The Fifth Letter of the Alphabet" (originally titled "Take a Small 'e'"), "Mamma"
Wind: "Son-In-Law"
Window: "Like February"

Cover design based on a print by Nancy Dahlstrom

The CSU Poetry Center expresses its gratitude to the Ohio Arts Council for a grant which aided the publication of this book.

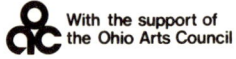
With the support of the Ohio Arts Council

Copyright © 1980 by Valery Nash
ISBN: 0-914946-16-1
Library of Congress Catalog No. 79-55445
Distributed by NACSCORP, Inc., Oberlin, Ohio, and by *Field*, Oberlin College, Oberlin, Ohio

For my parents, Edith and Leland

CONTENTS

I. Facts
    The Distance..10
    The Stones at Devereux 11
    The Red Queen 12
    The Fifth Letter of the Alphabet 14
    The Last Child at Home 15
    The Bike 16
    Working for Doctor No...17
    The Extermination of the Shy................................18
    Facts: a Father's Death 19

II. Your List of Errands
    To Frame My Windows 24
    E.L.C..25
    At Eighty..26
    Rue de Monceau 27
    Your "Companions"...28
    The Smell 29
    You Introduce Me to Your Twin............................30
    The Floral Dress...31
    Mamma..32

III. The Fire I Teach Her
    Departure of the Youth..34
    Like February 35
    Patterning 36
    My Child..38
    Above, on Their Thrones, Slept the King and the Queen 39
    Witch Words 40
    The Woman Who Once Played God 42
    Son-In-Law..44
    Ilsebil Desirous of Stars and Planets 46

IV. The Grey Cow
    Absence 50
    Traveller 54
    Winter House..55
    In Silks...56
    The Angle of Reflection.......................................57
    Surprise Party Songs 58
    In Our Sixties...60
    The Rowboat on the North Sea.............................62

I. Facts

THE DISTANCE

First, decide what to take along,
what liquid to store in your canteen.
Plan to pick up whatever you can
on the way. It'll be fresher.
Don't stand forever
thinking about what it tastes like.
Think about the walking. Think about your shoes.

Tonight the soles may be split: you'll need a new pair.
They were one useful thing you brought. Don't look
for talismans. Let your steps
spring sod or stone.

Do you remember, at dawn
a woman handed you sandwiches, pointed the way,
and how the hills looked warm with the sun behind them?
Forget "warm." Try to remember her face.
She was out early. She didn't think
you were odd to ask directions at 6 a.m.,
to travel that distance, or odd
to follow her guesses.
She had twenty years on you. Keep walking.

Of course, you're not alone. Make do
with travelling in a crowd and learn to live
with man-made things like stores, hobbies, a garden—
not only that wild one, but one somebody planted.

The main thing always
is to start early, appreciate
as neither achievement nor waste
the distance you've come.

Remember: she seemed to think
each village has its own character. Don't dwell
on her thoughts any longer. Think of your excellent shoes.

THE STONES AT DEVEREUX

                Anything   anything
                   What?   Anything

Whatwhat?
   running

back and forth   the little boys
   like flat-footed crows
      land over and into
         water
      shrieking

Grandmothers   wearing   bathing caps
  earflaps   turned up for a talk
hail   from the shore

  Early the little boys
    early high-pitched
     scent the morning air
with a fine oil of giggles and feathers

Off-shore fathers
    float apart and together
       their toes to the sky
     like rhythmical islands
              booming
fog warnings

   Saying what?   Anything
Whatwhat?   Anything

        The draining   pulling
        the stones clapping

THE RED QUEEN
a blind and aimless Fury
—Lewis Carroll

At fifty-five she wakes early,
punchy from wrestling with dawn
in that dark arena
where she always loses
yet still gets up,
sweaty with night terrors,
her graying hair coarse and wiry
and foul from cigarettes.

This bitch needs little food,
is massive on crackers and Camels,
Dubonnet, an occasional eclair,
Metrecal, carrot sticks.

What she ruminates tastes bitter
from the sour state of her smile,
caved cheeks and lips drawn down.
What happened to the rosebuds?

And where are her slim, girlish hands?
Broadened now, like a Russian's.
Where that soft, melodic voice?
Grown deeper, given to sudden oaths,
good-natured bossing,
loud humor, braying laughter,
tireless discourse:
the rant.

She polishes her house to mirrors,
cooks *Cordon Bleu*, stitches needlepoint,
forces charities, bludgeons club meetings,
paralyzes shopkeepers and friends.

From her chin sprout hairs
as vigorous as tusks.

Grown men tremble at her
and nubile girls are offended
by this heavyweight, still sparring
without title or partner.

THE FIFTH LETTER OF THE ALPHABET

The "e" is central. Ink it jet.
It is a nerve. Nest it in a net
of words. Let it spread
its ends in the jell.
That is its bed.

Needle it with feeling. It is a cell
receiving. It can hear.
It has a sense head.
It is an ear.

It is an ear that keeps
what it is fed.
Electric secrets
hum and shudder
in its small center.
It is a key.

Later the "e" repeats
in a new word, remembers
    secrets it has heard
    meanings it has said—
these are what it feels,
and it will tell.
Repeated, the letter peals
in circles and circles.
It is a bell.

THE LAST CHILD AT HOME
—for Mady

The last child at home
leaves the living room
where her parents' T.V. roars.

On the porch the air is warm.
Fireflies trace in the treetops
curly initials, messages
she follows but can't read.

She dreams she is the older sister:
Rose White with the yellow braids,
who always made them play school.
She dreams she is the second sister:
Rose Red with the long black hair,
who wouldn't tell her boyfriends' names.

The last child at home
stacks the dishwasher by herself
opens the windows, feeds the cat
leaves crumbs on all the counters.

A dream she has
of a frame house with low ceilings
of hot mornings, slamming doors
a blue car crammed with people.

She feels she is already old.
She feels she may be important.
She looks up her horoscope
and plots her evening on the movie page.

The last child at home
won't give away her heart.
She finds long novels in the library
and reads them after school
taking turns lying, one by one,
on every bed in the house.

THE BIKE

Fast first
at its own speed and her indignity
panting
striving to pedal
keep it
at that rate
across lawns and crazily driveways criss-crossing
the wheels listing
like dying hoops
and falls on the grass to stop

To get back on
must throw herself
at the teetering thing her sharp machine
over and over
till she finds
its pace and is off clownishly wobbling
and has no idea
how to pedal slowly
yet

WORKING FOR DOCTOR NO
What sort of man could inspire fear like that?

Perhaps it was the beautiful efficiency
of the Doctor's organization,
or the attraction of strict discipline,
the little luxuries that those on the payroll let show
like hints: a silk shirt, a bracelet, old wine
in unaccustomed shaking hands.

Awake each morning at dawn, tossing
searching his rum-soaked brain
for details of the evening before:
the chance word slipped at the Club;
sweating under the sheets
with always the image of two steel hands
the round room, the echoing dark voice.

Does Professor Dent remember the days
before he worked for Doctor No?
Does he dream of leaving the island
retiring with his nest egg
to pursue geological research?

He would still wake sweating, trying
to remember where he slipped up.
And could he ever be sure?

He is safer staying where terror
becomes a way of life
as well-oiled as any other,
where there's no need to wonder what he fears.

Now his days are rigidly prescribed.
The order at Crab Key:

>   There.
>   On the table.
>   Pick it up.

THE EXTERMINATION OF THE SHY

What of those who freeze at bay,
the white deer?
What will be so remarkable as their stillness?

With what replace
their astonishing swift flight
when they run from us and leap
to the ocean, to the moon?

Or the slowness the shy enjoy when they feel safe
looking up from slow-thinking
gazing, gazing at nothing
releasing their tentative steps,
where will we find such slowness?

FACTS: A FATHER'S DEATH

I.

This man has a fact in him, his death.
No longer does his daughter want to ask
if his life has meaning
or if he's honest with himself.

She offers him the paper,
asks what he wants to eat.
   Feel better now?
Every minute he falls off in nightmares
right under her eyes.

He is shaken by voices, by rumors.
Lies rise and break around him like an ocean,
   but the fact.

It's not the black brine he leaves in the sink
or the shrill talons of whispers
or anything he thinks he hears.
Nothing vague
is like it at all:

this hard nail
he cannot cough up.

II.

What is so true
as happiness? the book asks.
I know a true thing.

Also, of course, I remember.
Recollections are like the clothes
which hang in my closet.
I made each crease in them
and they smell of my body.
They smell of my tobacco.
But I chose them for wearing
not for believing in.

They line up, cold and thick
as effigies — my outdoor days, memories, joy,
the old plan for happiness—
as irrelevant as these clothes
I will not wear.

III.

My daughter's cat leaps with greeting
onto my blanket.
His thick gray plush kneads the wool.

I smooth my hand along his back.
His fur is as fresh and watery
as the winter air outside.

It is winter outside my window
where the garden is just a collection
of brown stalks stuck in frost.

The clear bone ache of that garden.

IV.

What is that little weasel thing
that thing beside the vase
moving its flame up and down?

He is gathering webs
of confusion from the air
and winding them carefully
over his gray hands,
so that she sees his fingers
looped by gray fibrous
dust.

He winds it and tosses it away
with distaste.

V.

Stamping his feet
in a little dance on the bathroom floor
as he tries to hoist his pajamas.
    Wait a minute. Wait, can't you?
    So *that's* how you do it. Now I've got it. Of course.
He is always astonished.
    O, you're *there*, are you?
    O, I see. You're another one. That makes four.
He never asks, but tells her, her eager messenger.

It is changing so fast.
    O, now I see.
Bumping into the chairs.
    So that's the new arrangement. Much better. So that's
    the *new* way.
His grin sharp and clean,
he is catching on.

Every minute
there is more for him to learn.

VI.

At death, he fastens his light eyes
on her face and she sees

something going out of his watch
and something going out of the ceiling light.

What she feels going out of the watch
and what she feels withdrawing from the light—

for a moment only she feels
this separate fact
as well as the facts remaining.

II. Your List of Errands

TO FRAME MY WINDOWS

She is making over my blue curtains in a dream.
I am calling, crying at her in fear.
Blindly, she lifts the cloth and tears each seam.

She moves like clockwork, as ritual, as a mime,
she lowers and lifts and stretches cloth to tear.
She is making over my blue curtains in a dream.

Across and across before her she shifts the hem
of my blue silk, which snakes around her chair.
Blindly, she lifts the cloth and tears each seam.

I want to stop her. I beat on walls, which seem
to stand between us. Moving, she cannot hear.
She is making over my blue curtains in a dream.

They are my curtains, woven with the theme
of my old days, and colored with my air.
Blindly, she lifts the cloth and tears each seam.

She shapes for my windows a fresh, billowing stream
of ruffles, but from cloth I cannot spare.
She is making over my blue curtains in a dream.
Blindly, she lifts the cloth and tears each seam.

E. L. C.

What are you listing?
You lift a page and look up from your desk.
Your shingled hair
stands straight as a rooster's comb,
old scribe, old clever one.

In your head what names
of books, of customers, addresses,
what plots and characters
under the light,
over the ledgers, the files
of the E.L.C. BOOK ORDERING SERVICE
you set up at home.

Old career girl, old bluestocking,
old Colette, old Gertrude Stein,
old brain, unlikely mother
to me or any child.
Skirting your light, your circle,
outside your spell,
I sidle behind your chair,
reach for your list of errands
and inch away.

Old Nod, old wise head, where you write
you are shrunken small with time;
your skin and hair are white and dry
and nearly blown away.
Your brow contracts,
you look up cocky and shrewd.
you mock, "Cheer up, Val! I'll let you go soon."

You total my bill, touch
your stamp to the ink pad
and roll it to print your sign.

AT EIGHTY

There is constant noise of wind
in your house
the air-conditioner is on

the slap of cards
against a board
your long falling-down rows
of solitaire

at night radio music enters
through black edges
around the windows
your favorite program is playing

shadows moving
over the wallpaper
approach, then part
as you turn your head

I see myself there on the carpet
pull out the books one by one
examine what someone has written

trying to catch
the look you hide
when you're alone

RUE DE MONCEAU

At night in Paris
with one light burning
you came back to my high-ceilinged room,

summoned perhaps
by all that city:
the windows of Notre Dame
with their blue secret,
the perfumed Frenchwomen
high-heeling past me
with bread under an arm
and your shrewd eyes,
the French you taught me,
the streets of flowers,
the small shops of childhood,
the warm nights, the fountains.

All you wanted
all you ever wanted
was to say you forgave me:
"It's all right, Val," and ask once more for love.

The steel of your touch,
your long arms holding,
the high lights flickering
lengthening, dimming
like Notre Dame,

the length of darkness.

YOUR "COMPANIONS"

Did they do as substitutes?
Were they so different?

Rose with her cretin snuffle,
coarse, angry mouth,
dirty, work-hardened hands,
loose gaze;

Klara's cracked face
as she handed you her messes,
calling them food, calling you Jew;

the whine of Edna's powders and creams and medicines;

or Ruby voodoo priestess brewing stale grease,
stealing your Scotch, lying on her fat bed
with her split feet up, never hearing you—

were they not like me?
with their deafness?
with their slack, resentful hands?

Rose reached out with my rough arm to push you;
Klara left my own smears of egg on your plates;
Edna complained in my own unending whine;
and Ruby slipped my fingers into your cash box.

Your four brute witches, Mother, howled at you
with my black tongue, to the end.

THE SMELL

Mother sloughed me off
like her black toe.
*That cold-hearted kid,
never coming around.
Forget her.*

When they cut off her toe, she said:
Take Val, too,
turned my picture to the wall.
*Those letters from Val
in the top drawer, burn them.*

Blackness rose up her flesh,
crept in from the sides.
One day a finger turned.

Love is all that counts, she said.
*I rest with my memories
and my three friends.*

Afterwards I went back,
stood with her friends in that room
looking for signs of rage,
looking at that bone face.

Mother, we're both cold now.

YOU INTRODUCE ME TO YOUR TWIN

Bea loomed first from a mirror
over your basin at camp:
rubber clown lips, red cheeks,
and frightwig of curls.

And how she laughed, joked, ragged,
called, *I was only teasing!*
called, *Can't you take it?*
in the schoolyard
after five o'clock
when everyone was gone.

The high wire fence
beside which a red ball bounces.
Bea center stage
pulling down her drawers,
showing where she was spanked.

In the monkeyfur of a wrap borrowed
for your June prom,
she whirled, bumped shoulders:
the dressmaker's waltz partner.

Bea is cross. She blackens.
Makes your hands fly like stings,
leaving welts on my flesh.

What does she ask of you?
When you speak to her,
she shrinks in your eye
to a lonely coat
held against the fence
by two winds,
its cloth maroon and gray
the school colors.

THE FLORAL DRESS

We knew you were dead
and under stone.
You knew it, I knew it—
so how were we there
walking through shops?

I saw, of course,
that your death had tired you,
yet you looked younger
than I remembered.
Your face seemed clearer,
your dress a darkness
of floral satin
with wide black belt,
shoes new and stylish.
You were graceful, tall,
an attractive presence.

You let me fill
your arms with gifts
   of painted china
     silk shoes with buckles
     long chiffon scarves

and, though at my house
your face looked puzzled
with a little worry
remembering death,
you let me say
that we were lucky
to sit together
for drinks on the couch

to know of your death
as two women, talking
as friends, and laughing
that bright afternoon
before you vanished.

MAMMA

The big woman
that my mother was
but that she never let be born
  sprawls in my head:

the sloppy breasts, all slopes
all jelly, the legs outthrust
under billowing stomach,
the big woman's smile
easy as sunlight, big woman's summer sweat
the flowered cotton dress a-gape
and stockings rolled halfway down.

My mother lived in corsets:
pushed up her breasts, waist in,
fastened herself together with hooks and eyes
(red patterns of furious pinches down her back)

and shrivelled finally under that all-in-one
to little nut-black puckerings
as fussy as her diets,
shrank squirrel-like and hidden.

In dreams I let her out.
I take out her seams like one of her old robes
till she sprawls her big shoulders
as wide as the sun over mountains.

In sleep, I sweat; I wait
for the slap of that big woman's hand
to fill my lungs with living.

III. The Fire I Teach Her

DEPARTURE OF THE YOUTH

They move off into exile
looking back at the Five Lands
where we are at home.

They go to an austere country
of flickering lights, a low sun,
continual wind.

They are well-taught. They know how
to allot provisions justly
to hunt and fish
to converse and exchange wisdom
to tame fear
to make moss edible
to stifle the noise from the forest
to build shelter against dreams.
They know how to sleep.

Their exile
will make the soil of home more rich.
Our days all swell with the harvest
of memories they have lost.

They are boarding the ships. They are calling.
At an hour as wide as noon
they are pulling up the gangways
with one accord.

They do not seek to stay.
They are not greedy.
They leave to each of us
a life like each of theirs.

LIKE FEBRUARY

The woman is all belly.
At night she rocks it, cradles
her canteloupe, her pearl.

And the stories she rocks to herself
are of virgin births,
hysterical pregnancies,
of Mexican squaws who drop their infants
like melons in hot fields
studded with crops like hearts.

She is a Vermeer lady
in wimple and furred cloak
with hands at rest on the table
of an enormous womb.
Her fingers fine as whalebone
lattice the swelling crescent.

A hundred nights her thick cat comes
to lay an ear against her clock.
Round as the moon, she straddles
her husband with its beating.

She dreams of passion hidden
under velvet stomachers,
of sin shrouded in veils
behind monastic walls,
of coffins too full to close.

The woman cannot believe
that anything is born.
She dreams her seed is planted
too deep to grow,
that embryonic stems
tangle in her dark,
turned to whitest treasure
buried for keeping.

PATTERNING

To stimulate undamaged brain cells to take over the function of the damaged cells...three adults must move the child's body in rhythmic exercise patterns...

We are all in labor with her here
all sweating and trying
She whines on the padded table
in bones and outgrown pajamas

> They are in and out
> I can see yellow light when they hold it there
> noisy and large   they pull my arms and legs
> on crooked wheels
> and I whine   I will whine

She has shrunk to the shape of her bones
locked on springs
too taut for flesh
We are turning her hard locked springs

> Each one is different
> sometimes I eat their skin like soup or leaves
> long hands warm along my face
> they are in and out like lights

Her rollicking blind eyes like fairy boats
rock and curl and tinsel on themselves
blown brown with lashes
black as waves
We are turning her out of sleep

> I will not move alone
> they pinch   I hear myself
> cry   I will cry
> whine   I will whine

We pinch her arms and legs to make her crawl
Push   little piggy   Try to make her laugh

        Sometimes they make me laugh or I forget
        sudden I feel it breathe
        across the water

We are all turning her harsh in labor

        everything suddenly
        going by itself
        won't wait for me   listen

MY CHILD

It is a small, square scene
by a darkness
where I hold her squarely.

What is in her body?
fluted ribs,
chords of flesh.

And a skin like crying.
Daughter a sorrow word.

In her keeping,
cut into her chords inside:
all that is grief, ever grieved for.

What is in her body?
a crying.
In this dark scene I bind her.

ABOVE, ON THEIR THRONES, SLEPT THE KING AND THE QUEEN

We return to our living room together.
You hair is disordered. From your brow rise questions.
You put your hand to your crown. You shake your head.
   Where did we place the princess?
   Did we leave her enough money?

You have just been to the mirror. You return distressed.
   I have witnessed murder.

My two hands rise to your cheeks. I am full of comfort:
our familiar lists, our calculations.
   Remember, love, you burned the spindles.

You sit in the big wing-chair by the fire.
As you read, you nod. Your lips are pale as frost.
   Your head is heavy against me.

You are stumbling through a desert. You go slower.
Your eyes are bewildered. Sometimes they are cunning.
   I read myself in your eyes.

When you are asleep, I walk in secret.
Airs stir in our hall; the curtains shudder.
Dust sifts across the stones of our old house.
   Only twelve golden plates; the hedge of thorn.
   The fire leaps from the meat; the little door.

We have buried a sleeping princess.
The walls are crying.

WITCH WORDS

I, like the children, am in the forest
and not safe
though in my gingerbread house.

I, too, am hungry.
My sugary roof and windows
no longer satisfy.
Only child flesh will fatten.

And I shiver.
Gretel, fetch axe, fetch wood.
Gretel, why are you so slow?

Over and over, it is winter:
the woodcutter, his bare larder
the wise birds choosing the crumbs
and the hunger that brings her here.

Over and over, it happens:
Gretel's daze, her dreaming step
her arms hanging down
as flat as fish.

Once again she finds me stumbling
around the rooms, half blind.
Gretel's cheeks are bright as apples.

She approaches weeping, grieving
for her caged brother, her love.
Gretel, you must light the oven.
Gretel, let me show you how.

Once again she doesn't know I planned it:
Gretel's sharp hands, her strong thrust
and afterwards, her smile.

Oh, how frightfully I howl.
The black forest rises, howls with me
roars with the fire I teach her.

THE WOMAN WHO ONCE PLAYED GOD

At her dinner table
she gave herself away.
Under the buzz of talk
the lamps softly shaded
she handed round her life
in wine and casseroles.

In her living room
she gave herself away.
The hands of her affection
spread like wings
over the difficult puppets
who sprawled on her sofas.
She could feel them on her arms
drinking her sweetness.
They pulled on her nerves like bees.

Her children and guests moved close.
She felt herself devoured
by smiles.

At her birthday party
she gave herself away.
She let down her long hair
let it flow forth like rivers
along which her children went sailing.
She was lovely to the ends of her fingers
her hands firm with rings glinting
gifted, musical.
Her sympathy quivered like stars.

She woke up one morning
to find she had vanished.
Wind clattered through her rafters
tore round her splintering walls.
Beetles climbed the bare supports.

Ah, this is what I meant, she said.
She loved them, she was absent.
They loved her, she was gone.

She left no reflection in the water.
She cast no shadow on the field.
Her body no longer blocked the sun
or shone in the sky's mirror.

SON-IN-LAW

Translated into kin
he enters my house
with a touch of flattery
smiles and fond eyes.
He teases a blush on my arms, my cheeks
and the clatter of love down my old stairs.

At my spread table
the newlyweds are merry
pouring out wine
leaving things:
his twisted cigarette
long hairs on surfaces.

In the curtained bedroom
they whisper, joke
stroking each other with wit
finding fault, laughing.

I am bent with picking up
with listening at doors.

Where I enter rooms
they slip quietly away.
Where I polish the mahogany
they plot a new style.
Where I bake them feasts
they are sorry, and sickened.

What is my son-in-law thinking?
He is polite
but cool. His eyes veer away:
something he is too tactful to see.

A traitor he is, masked in smiles
a confidence man who is stealing

features from my portraits
cornerstones from my walls
history from my antiques
leaving a shrine of sticks.

Black henbane I stir in his food.
Under my mattress a doll
of clay. He is losing flesh.

I will raise my hand,
I will bring down my home
on the son-in-law
related to me not by blood
but lust.

ILSEBIL DESIROUS OF STARS AND PLANETS
My wife, Ilsebil, must have her own will.
—The Fisherman's Wife

She rubs a strong arm
across weak eyes.
In her dream she was swimming.

Again the rude sun got up
before she said it could.
Again her palace's marble
is veined with patterns of ocean
which flow as she turns her head.

Her stiff hair escapes the crown.
Her golden skirt hikes to one side,
too tight after last night's feasting.

She summons handmaidens, claps her palms.
The casements open; she commands
far over the coast, the cliffs, the towns,
the distant sea,
the surf which rises to her, billows, bows,
curtseys and laughs.

Perch on my wrist, she tells the sun.
It flicks its tail in her rings,
sears a hole like a silver coin
in the center of her gaze.
When her husband gets back, she will complain.
There will be something he can do.

Affairs of state, the ordering
of tapestries from merchants make her snore.
In her sleep there are streams of mackerel
that touch each other with their lips.

She summons footmen: the strongest climbers
with the longest arms to net that moon,
four-masted ships to trawl the sea
for the glittering path it trails there.
She will gather this for her train.

But the smug moon sails
on another course
dragging its own gold fin,
and will not admit she is right,
and will not return her love.

When her husband gets back, she will tell him
how the sun and the moon evade her,
give her nightmares of cutting fish
in some old cottage by the waves.

Enthroned, she faces her mirror,
pretends she is the sun.
You do as I say, she tells herself
and can see from her glow, she is ready.

IV. The Grey Cow

*He said "exactly" for "except": "All the cows
have come home exactly the grey cow."*
—Isak Dinesen

ABSENCE

I.

The door blows open
I know it is you
one of your sudden returns

Nothing else arrives
so abrupt, so sure of welcome

Wind surrounds my house
comes from all sides at once
wakes me at night, raising spring

clamps my door shut
I thrust my shoulder to it
but glass will not shift

When I turn away
again the door flies open
This is how you enter

II.

Told to keep silence
for the sake of the village
for the salvage of the old house—
we entwine, just fingers

One word only each hour, or one sentence
We come to prefer the banks of streams
lying and kissing

Kissing also we may seldom do
The white sky comes down to our home
The house making windows
to fill our absence

III.

Wanting to live inside your life
your nice clothes

be buttoned in
the corduroy of your jacket

to flush with your fine cheeks
sting red with your winter lips
when you bite them, feel
the sharp white edge

to wait there lounging
back against the stairwell's
green wallpaper
at ease smiling, or restless

to run untired
like skin under silk
inside your elegant thoughts

IV.

You sit up late
I am near the door, I hear your page
turn
the wind
lifting the wet-fallen leaves outside

You in your room alone reading

I go down the hall
and pause, I can feel
how happy you are
your thoughts
there on the wind's current

I hear
the time turn idly in your room

V.

You are somewhere around the house
sleeping or waking
not in this room
but another
working at your books
turning white papers under the lamp
looking up
keeping your place with one finger

Or you are on the bed
sprawled huge
lost to time

You should be easy to find
where your clothes, your letters
were tossed down

A car streams up the gravel outside
and passes without stopping

VI.

Where I look but can't find you
you make your way
grazing the corner
                after I leave
pausing quietly by the window
in the kitchen tapping the wall

For a long time you may have sat
legs crossed, chin sunken
in the old wing chair
before I came in

You rise
        stretching and growing
Your suit spreads up like a stain
of shadow against the light

Your steps crash through the house
        filling it
                vanishing

TRAVELLER

I am younger than you
I am thinner
My pockets are full of holes

I am sitting in a bus station
at three a.m.
somewhere north of Chicago

I speak less than you
I am nervous
Outside, the snow

is crusted along
the dark highway
The bus is late

I light a cigarette
and start to drum my fingers
on the bench

I am more private than you
more solitary
Clusters of stars

pass through the holes in my pockets
pass through my jacket's lining
and through the soles of my shoes

My jacket is threadbare
My flesh smells of nothing
of snow

By morning
I will sleep like a child
in the back of the bus

WINTER HOUSE

Sloth becomes refined
almost to exercise,
as I hold motionless
stubborn
in the hot room,
watching the stove burn
the food I have tended,
hearing my heart louden
to fury against the steam,
fragrant with food and furnace,
that I must breathe.
Only the small soul,
sleeping under ice
out in the shrunken dark
where stars wheel and freeze,
is deep enough.

IN SILKS

Done rapidly
like a thief
raking up small, round
gems by hundreds

with the fine tips
of lean fingers.
A sudden sweep
a flash of teeth.

We become fast
and supple, in silks
at a game of jacks
this certain, foreign.

THE ANGLE OF REFLECTION

Sun so strong it knocked me down
I lay on a tilted lawn
while fingers of sun
crept into my clothes and head

Tried to get up it knocked me down
elbowed my face
I tried to climb up its beam
hot finger by hot finger

Climbed the sun and sat on its head
among dark curly hair
up where the thoughts knot
with a smell of wire singeing

Looked down on the world
and saw myself
glass on a glass lawn

SURPRISE PARTY SONGS

I.

Susan will be there and Ruth
standing in front of their chairs
smiling with expectation of my surprise

at a party in the old frame house
built high above the pier

Lights in the center
and shadows on the wall
black tents, pointed and huge

*I know where I'm going
and I know who's going with me*

Susan, Ruth, Sue, Barbara
forming a circle
smiling, coming forward
giving me presents
a room full of guests

Each gives me a testimonial
certificate that I know her
Straight chairs around the walls
beneath the house the tide

*Go in and out the window
Now come and face your partner*

Around, around
we are taking hands
Each of them looks at me
smiles in eyes, their hands
reaching me my best dreams
the ones I can never remember
out of the waters of sleep

II.

They hand me certificates, rolled and tied
I open them — each is a report card
On the report cards are nothing but A's

Fly-away A's like bows
like kites like empty frames
like houses on stilts like open hats
sharp pencil stitches

My face is flushed
my hair is combed
I am in the circle
I am going to speak

The room rocks
the house on its pilings
We rush to the corners
the center for balance
Their bodies shunted white against the walls
skirts and arms, black bruises and long wet hair
Thank you, thank you, thank you — I grasp my prizes

I know who's going with me
but the dear knows who I'll marry

IN OUR SIXTIES

In our home
gray with sea
and lashed by light rain
no one watches us.

Its disciplined yard
is fenced and deep-earthed.
Here you are planting rows—
of peas?   of lettuces?

no child questions this crop
and I neglect to ask.
Nor do we remember
the names of those dull birds
that flap behind your rake

or if we knew them once
or if they have come before.

Inside we set our board
and take the meal swiftly
with no one to litter the cloth
no one to resent
the lateness of dinner
the bread soured by damp.

Inserted unasked
through a cold mouth in our door,
the mail piles, drifts
like snow over the sill.
It is all addressed
to you, to me.

At night, the sea
moves stronger in our ears
and bolder by my side

and the audience
turns away from us
towards some spectacle
which they watch
totally absorbed.

The applause they lift
between palms white with salt
thunders beyond our home.

THE ROWBOAT ON THE NORTH SEA
—for Henry

It is like
walking together to the same step:
your schedule, my schedule
the minutes we allow together.

It is like my asking:
What do you think that reminds me of?
and your answers
being right, though wrong.

Only I am not sure
and never look too closely
at the grayness of your cheek,
the line of white across your brow.

Two riders are in the rowboat,
their faces hidden, blurred by mist,
only dimly seen this time of year
in the softness and darkness of December.

We would not know a horizon was there
were it not for the boat that hangs
not very far out
motionless in the fog—

where all is purple and gray,
a cup riding low waves:
two riders, and their lines
in a sea almost drained of light.

It is dusk all afternoon;
you and I pretending to look for rocks,
not mentioning our joy
in our cold walks, these latitudes.